Printed in China by Toppan

Paperback Edition
23 22 21 20 19   5 4 3 2 1

Published by
Gibbs Smith
P.O. Box 667
Layton, Utah 84041
1.800.835.4993 orders
www.gibbs-smith.com

Designed by Rita Sowins / Sowins Design
Gibbs Smith books are printed on either recycled, 100% post-consumer
waste, FSC-certified papers or on paper produced from sustainable PEFC-
certified forest/controlled wood source. Learn more at www.pefc.org.

Library of Congress Cataloging-in-Publication Data

Snow, Virginia Brimhall.
  Winter walk / Virginia Brimhall Snow. —— First edition.
    pages cm
  ISBN 978-1-4236-3747-9 (hardcover)
  ISBN 978-1-4236-5392-9 (paperback)
1. Snowflakes——Juvenile literature. 2. Snow——Juvenile literature.
3. Animals——Wintering——Juvenile literature. I. Title.
  QC926.37.S66 2014
  508.2——dc23
                    2014000655

*To Mom, who
shared her love of
reading, children,
nature and all good
things with me.*

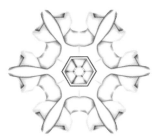

Winter Walk

VIRGINIA BRIMHALL SNOW

GIBBS SMITH
TO ENRICH AND INSPIRE HUMANKIND

holly

I went for a walk with
my grammy today.
The **fluffy white snow**
urged me to *play*.

snowdrop

snowflake

icicles

I stuck out my *tongue*,
caught a snowflake and giggled,
Then **stretched** my arms wide,
plopped down and *wiggled*.

deciduous tree

fox

Against the bright snow all the
bare trees looked dead.

"Those trees without leaves
are *asleep*," Grammy said.

"Through these cold months
many animals *rest*, too.

raccoon

bear

They **hibernate** underground until winter is through."

"Why is this tree **green**, Grammy, when others are brown?"

"Because evergreens have *needles* that stay green year-round."

pine tree

pinecone

blue spruce
branch

blue spruce
pinecone

At a fat, bluish pine tree,
I brushed off some snow,

Then picked up some *pinecones*
that had fallen below.

ponderosa
branch

I found another green tree;
the **needles** were long.

Its pinecones were very
big, prickly and *strong.*

deer

Silently through the trees
slipped a long-legged deer.

snowshoe hare

I spotted a **white bunny**
with *big floppy* ears.

chickadee

acorn

On a high branch perched a *wee chickadee.*

"Ducks and geese **fly** south, so *why* didn't he?"

cardinal

"Some birds don't **migrate**, they stay here instead.

They eat *seeds* from our feeders," my grammy said.

bird feeder

snowflake

Tiny white flakes drifted
onto my nose.
They covered my
lashes and *fingers* and *toes*.

chestnut

"Every snowflake is **unique**.
Each one has six sides."

I couldn't see that on my
mittens, though I tried.

snowball

ivy

I scooped up more flakes
to *pack* into a **ball**,

And we built a fine **snowman**
in no time at all.

winterberries

He had **rocks** for his eyes.
Our sticks gave him arms.

His mouth was of *berries*
and a scarf kept him warm.

snowman

He seemed to be *watching* us as we trudged in.

I hope to go back out and **play** with him again.

Six-Sided Paper Snowflakes

YOU WILL NEED:

- Paper
- Scissors

DIRECTIONS:

1. Fold one corner of your paper diagonally to the opposite side making a triangle with a tail. (Skip steps 1 and 2 if the paper is already square.)

2. Cut off the tail.

3. Unfold the triangle and fold the paper into a rectangle.

4. Fold the rectangle in half and unfold.

5. Fold the right side of the paper to meet the centerfold; unfold.

6. Fold the bottom left corner up to meet the last fold, dot to dot.

7. Fold the bottom right corner up over the left side, dot to dot.

8. Fold in half along the dotted line.

9. Cut across the dotted line.

10. Cut a design in the final triangle.

11. Unfold and see your beautiful snowflake.

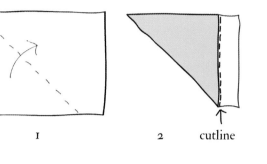

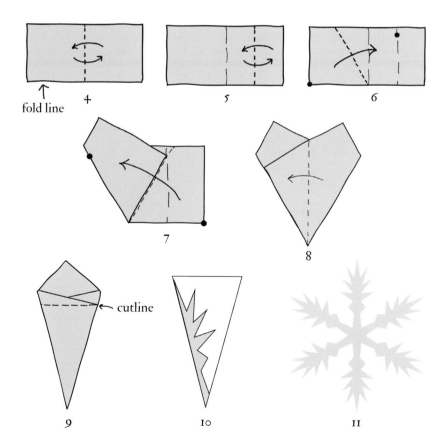

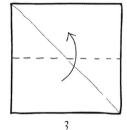

Pinecone Bird Feeder

YOU WILL NEED:

- Birdseed
- Pie tin
- 1 piece string, yarn or ribbon, cut about 18 inches long
- 1 large, open pinecone
- Scissors
- Butter knife
- Peanut butter

DIRECTIONS

1. Pour some birdseed into the pie tin.
2. Tie one end of the string tightly around the pinecone near its end.
3. Spread peanut butter all over the pinecone with a butter knife. (This is the fun, messy part.)
4. Roll the sticky pinecone in the birdseed until it is well covered. The pinecone is now a bird feeder.
5. Hang the bird feeder on a small branch away from the trunk of the tree so other creatures won't eat it.
6. Enjoy watching the different birds that come to eat.

Winter Trivia

1. Snowflakes have six sides because of the way water molecules bond as they freeze.

2. Water expands as it freezes, while most liquids shrink as they cool into solids. This makes ice less heavy than water, which causes it to float. If ice didn't float, many bodies of water would freeze solid. Fish and animals living there would not survive.

3. Snow looks white because sunlight is bounced around by the many tiny crystals of water that make up snow. All of the different colors of light that make up sunlight are reflected back and combine to look white.

4. Snowdrops (a flower) can push through the snow to blossom in late winter.

5. When animals hibernate, their body temperature drops and their heart rate slows way down. This conserves their energy so they can live off their body fat until they wake up in the spring.

6. Many different kinds of animals and insects hibernate. Some animals that hibernate are turtles, mice, skunks, raccoons, bears, squirrels, snakes, bees and snails. Some hibernate in caves, and others hibernate underground or in trees.

7. Pinecones are the seedpods of pine trees. They open to spread their seeds when it is warm and dry. The needles of pine trees and many other evergreens are their leaves. These needles stay on the tree year-round.

8. Deciduous trees lose their leaves in the fall and appear dead during the winter. They rest during the cold months, much like animals hibernating.

9. The fur on some animals, like the snowshoe hare, changes to white in the winter. This camouflage helps them to hide from predators.

10. Many birds fly thousands of miles to spend the winter in a warmer climate. Other birds, like the cardinal and chickadee, spend their winters in cold climates.

11. Gray squirrels bury nuts in a scattered pattern to eat during winter. They often forget some of the nuts. Many of the forgotten ones sprout and grow into new trees.